JAMESTOWN

MW00717101

THE
CONTEMPORARY
READER

VOLUME 2, NUMBER 3

Editorial Director: Cindy Krejcsi
Executive Director: Marilyn Cunningham
Editor: Christine Kelner
Editorial Services Manager: Sylvia Bace
Market Development Manager: Mary Sue Dillingofski
Design Manager: Ophelia M. Chambliss
Production Manager: Margo Goia

ACKNOWLEDGMENT
"How to Survive Anything" adapted from "How to Survive Anything"
by Jeffrey Csatari, *Men's Health Magazine,* June1994.
Copyright © 1994 by Rodale Press, Inc. Adapted by permission of
Men's Health Magazine. All rights reserved.

ISBN: 0-89061-828-3

Published by Jamestown Publishers,
a division of NTC/Contemporary Publishing Group, Inc.
4255 West Touhy Avenue,
Lincolnwood (Chicago), Illinois, 60646-1975, U.S.A.
© 1998 NTC/Contemporary Publishing Group, Inc..

9 WKT 0 9 8 7 6 5 4 3 2

CONTENTS

Pronunciation Key

ă	mat	o͞o	food
ā	date	o͝o	look
â	bare	ŭ	drum
ä	father	yo͞o	cute
ĕ	wet	û	fur
ē	see	*th*	then
ĭ	tip	th	thin
ī	ice	hw	which
î	pierce	zh	usual
ŏ	hot	ə	alone
ō	no		open
ô	law		pencil
oi	boil		lemon
ou	loud		campus

The Chunnel Under the Sea

*Why build a tunnel under
the English Channel?*

1   In one sense, England is part of Europe.
English history is closely tied to that of
Europe. The music and art of England have
strong links with Europe. England also trades
with all the nations of Europe.

2   In another sense, England has not been
part of Europe. After all, England is part of an
island. The English Channel divides it from
the rest of Europe. Getting from England to
the rest of Europe and back required a boat
or plane ride.

3   That, however, is no longer true. A land
route now links England to France. In 1994,
the Channel Tunnel opened. Nicknamed the
Chunnel, it is 31 miles long—the world's
longest underwater tunnel.

**The English Channel is the body of water that separates
England from France.**

An Old Idea

4 Before the last ice age, England was connected to France by land. When the ice melted, about 8,000 years ago, the sea level rose and created the English Channel. That body of water made travel between England and Europe much more difficult.

5   By 1751, people were thinking about building a tunnel under the channel. In the early 1800s, Emperor Napoleon I of France made plans to build a dual[1] tunnel. But war broke out and killed his dream.

6   Since then, other dreamers have wanted to build a tunnel. But people's fears on both sides of the channel always stopped them. Some people thought that armies might use such a tunnel to invade. Others worried that a tunnel would help the spread of disease.

7   At last, in 1986, such fears were put aside. People on both sides of the channel really wanted a tunnel. So the French and the English agreed to work together on the project. They figured that the tunnel would cost $7 billion. They planned to open the tunnel in 1993.

---

[1] dual: double

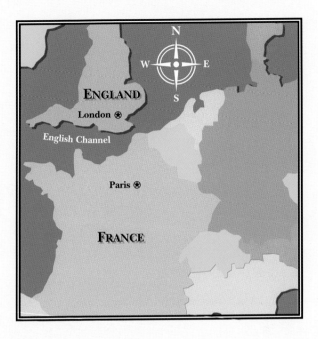

8   Building the tunnel was a huge project. New problems came up that surprised the planners. They had extra work to do. So, in the end, the Chunnel cost $16 billion. And it opened a year later than planned.

Building the Chunnel

9   It was a challenge to build such a tunnel. Engineers built special boring[2] machines, called *moles*. These moles were huge. Each one weighed 1,500 tons and was longer than two football fields. The machines did the

---

[2] boring: hole-digging

4 THE CHUNNEL UNDER THE SEA

4 THE CHUNNEL UNDER THE SEA

Machines like this drilled out clay inside the tunnel before the "moles" went to work.

job—their massive[3] blades made holes that were perfectly round. They dug out about 245 million cubic feet of earth. At one point, the moles dug 148 feet below the seabed of the English Channel.

10   One group of workers started in France. Another started in England. Their goal was to make the tunnels meet under the English Channel. When they did meet, in 1990, everyone was amazed. The meeting point of the tunnels was off the right measure by just eight inches.

---

[3] massive: huge

11   The project took 10,000 workers to complete. Their job was wet, muddy, and cold. It was also dangerous. Eight English workers and 2 French workers died on the job. That safety record was not too bad. When Japan built the world's second-longest tunnel, 30 workers lost their lives.

The Chunnel Design

12   The Chunnel is really made up of three tunnels. Two of them have train tracks. The trains on one set of tracks run from England to France. The trains on the other set run from France to England. The third tunnel

This 1987 photo shows workers at the French end of the Chunnel.

is a service tunnel with a road. Trucks use this third passageway to carry supplies and workers. The workers keep the other two tunnels in good shape.

13   The trains themselves are much larger than average-sized trains. In fact, they are the widest trains ever built. They need room enough to carry cars, buses, and trucks as well as people. Despite their size, these trains zip through the Chunnel at nearly 90 miles per hour. The passenger trains are even faster. They go 186 miles per hour.

14   Two locomotives, one in the front and one in the back, run each train. Most locomotives have one engine. But each Chunnel locomotive has six of them. That totals twelve engines for each train!

15   There is a good reason for having many engines. Europe uses three different electric systems. So there has to be one engine for each. Each system also needs a second engine as a backup. No one wants to get stuck in the Chunnel because of a power failure.

Dealing with Problems

16   The Chunnel has had a few problems. One was heat. No one thought the tunnels would

The Eurostar Chunnel train looks very much like a sea creature.

get hot. But the trains speeding back and forth made the tunnels very hot. So the builders had to add an air-conditioning system. This added another $200 million to the cost of the project. The new system is large enough to cool 6,000 homes.

17   Some people worried about floods. They didn't want to drown if the Chunnel sprang a leak. Builders say there is really no danger of large leaks because the tunnel is far below the seabed. What's more, the tunnel walls are made of reinforced [rē ĭn fôrst´] concrete and cast iron. Fire, however, is a more likely danger. Once again, the builders planned ahead. Any fire that breaks out will not

spread. Automatic doors slam shut to contain the blaze. Then foam will spray on the fire to put it out.

The Way to Go

18 Is it faster to fly across the English Channel than to use the Chunnel? Yes, but the Chunnel is better able to do the job. Airports in London and Paris are far from the centers of those cities. They are often plagued[4] by flight delays. Chunnel travelers can hop into their cars, drive onto a train, and be across the channel in 35 minutes. Or they can ride from downtown London to downtown Paris. The passenger train takes only three hours.

19   Each year more people use the Chunnel. Soon they will forget that it was once just a dream. ◆

---

[4] plagued: bothered

QUESTIONS

1. In what ways is England part of Europe?
2. What fears stopped people from building a tunnel sooner?
3. What problems did the builders of the Chunnel face?
4. What have builders done to make the Chunnel safe and comfortable?
5. How is travel by the Chunnel better than travel by air?

Chicago's Killer Heat Wave

How can heat be deadlier than fire?

1   The city of Chicago has seen its share of horrors. The Great Chicago Fire of 1871 killed 250 people. In 1903, a fire broke out in a theater and claimed 600 lives. Then there was the *Eastland* disaster in 1915. That ship tipped over on the Chicago River. More than 800 people drowned.

2   All of these were dramatic[1] events. Some disasters, though, are different: they are quiet. No one yells or screams for help, yet death has paid a visit. A killer heat wave is that kind of disaster. People die quietly, here and there. But added up, the number of deaths reaches the disaster point. The heat

---

[1] dramatic: striking or forceful

The heat wave of 1995 turned Chicago into a city of death.

wave that hit Chicago in 1995 was that kind of disaster. It killed more than 700 people.

Really Hot Weather

3   The stifling[2] heat arrived on July 12. Ninety degrees Fahrenheit [făr´ən hīt] is hot. The National Weather Service calls three days of such heat a heat wave. People can die in constant 90-degree heat. But this heat went far beyond 90 degrees. On July 13, the temperature hit 104 degrees in the city. The next day it

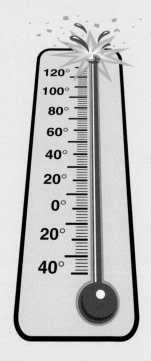

was still high—100 degrees. This record heat lasted for five days!

4   Hot weather is worse in a city than in the country. Why? A city has fewer trees and shady places. A city's many buildings and paved roads just soak up the heat. Also, cars and factories make heat of their own.

---

[2] stifling: hot and sticky

Some Reasons

5   Chicago has had heat waves in the past. Why did this one kill so many people? Of course, one important reason was that the heat was intense.[3] Besides that, though, was the high dew point—76 degrees. The dew point is a measure of humidity, or the amount of water in the air. Any time the dew point rises above 70 degrees Fahrenheit, the weather causes great discomfort. The high dew point made it hard for people to cool their bodies in the normal way, by sweating.

6   Heat and humidity work together in the same way as cold and wind. That is why winter weather reports give the wind chill as well as the true temperature. High winds make cold temperatures feel colder than they really are. In the same way, a high dew point makes fierce heat fiercer. In Chicago, the 100-degree heat felt more like 120 degrees.

The Old and the Poor

7   The killer heat wave was hardest on the old and the poor. Older people do not handle heat well. Their bodies do not sweat easily.

---

[3] intense: strong

Another problem is the medicines many old people take. Some of these drugs, meant to reduce body fluids, quickly dehydrate[4] [dē hī´drāt] the body. Too much water loss raises body heat.

8   Couldn't these people just turn on an air conditioner? Well, many poor people don't own one. Others don't even own fans. Some people who did have air conditioners or fans did not turn them on. Why not? They were trying to keep down the charges on their electric bills.

9   Many poor people live in neighborhoods with a lot of crime. They lock their doors and windows. Some people even nail their windows shut. This action might keep out thieves, but it keeps heat in. It killed many people in Chicago who were home alone.

10   Not all of the victims were old. Two three-year-old toddlers died in a daycare center's van. On their way to the center, they had fallen asleep in the back of the van. No one

---

[4] dehydrate: lose water; become dry

missed them when the other eight children aboard got out. The van's windows were rolled up, and the two children died from the heat. The heat inside that van might have been as high as 190 degrees!

So Many Deaths

11 On a normal day, the medical examiner in Chicago sees about 15 bodies. But the days of the heat wave were not normal. So many bodies came to the morgue[5] [môrg] that soon there was no room left. The extra bodies had to be stored in seven refrigerated vans.

12 Did the heat kill all of those people? Edmund Donoghue, the medical examiner, had no doubts. He said, "All of these people would have survived if not for the heat." Many of the bodies were hot to the touch. Some had body temperatures as high as 108 degrees. At such temperatures, said one doctor, "the brain is [in fact] fried."

Can It Happen Again?

13 Health officers across the country paid attention to what happened in Chicago.

---

[5] morgue: a place where the bodies of people found dead are taken

They studied ways to prevent such a tragedy in the future.

14   The National Weather Service is creating a heat-warning system. This system will watch for conditions like those that hit Chicago. The service hopes to warn cities two days before dangerous heat hits them. This kind of warning would give local workers time to act.

15   As people in Chicago learned, it is not enough to set up cooling shelters. People need to be told where the shelters are and when to go to them. City workers must go door-to-door to warn older people.

16   Also friends and relatives of old people should check up on them. Those who live alone and those who are ill need special care.

17   The Chicago heat wave of 1995 showed how weather can kill. What health workers learned can prevent many deaths from heat in the future. ◆

These children made keeping cool a part of their summer fun.

QUESTIONS

1. How does the heat wave of 1995 compare
   with some of Chicago's other disasters?
2. What made this heat wave much worse
   than most heat waves?
3. Why were old people an easy target for
   the heat?
4. Why were so many of the heat victims
   also poor?
5. How can this kind of disaster be avoided?

Black army units, like the one shown here, could not join the Union army until 1863. By then the country was at the midpoint of the Civil War.

BLACK SOLDIERS

UNSUNG HEROES

*How did black soldiers help save
the Union during the Civil War?*

1 The Civil War, fought between 1861 and
1865, threatened to break up the
United States. It began as a
struggle over states' rights. But
in 1863, President Abraham
Lincoln changed history. He
made the war a fight to end
slavery. Black soldiers played a
key role in this fight.

**Abraham Lincoln
(1809–1865)**

Not Wanted

2 Most people felt that a war would end in a
few weeks or months. Some free black men
offered to join the Union army. But they were

turned down. Union leaders did not think the army needed them.

3   The hope of a short war ended soon after the Battle of Bull Run. The North lost this battle, fought three months after the war started. Such defeat meant that the war could last for years. Still, there was no call for blacks to join the army. Northern leaders were sure that white soldiers could win the war alone.

Black Volunteers

4   If the army wouldn't have them, maybe blacks could help the cause in other ways.

Many black volunteers worked on defenses for the Union army.

In large numbers, they stepped forward to do many kinds of work. They built roads and forts. They carried supplies to the front lines. In short, these volunteers did whatever they could to help the Union cause.

5   But blacks were still not allowed to fight for the Union. That rule began to change in 1862. The war had been going badly for the North. In Kansas, a white abolitionist[1] [ăb ə lĭsh´ə nĭst] named Jim Lane took action. He set up two black regiments.[2] Even though they were not part of the regular Union army, they fought bravely in two small battles. "[The black soldiers] fought like tigers," said one Southerner.

Fighting for Freedom

6   On New Year's Day of 1863, President Abraham Lincoln issued[3] his Emancipation Proclamation [ĭ măn sə pā´ shən prŏk lə mā´ shən]. It was a bold move. It freed the slaves in the South. That, by itself, meant little. Since the war was still on, Lincoln could not force the South to obey.

---

[1] abolitionist: one who works to stop slavery
[2] regiment: an army unit
[3] issued: published or sent out

But in another sense, the proclamation meant everything. It gave the Civil War an added purpose: the fight was now to end slavery.

7   The proclamation also allowed black men to join the Union army. Black soldiers could now fight in separate units under white officers. Many blacks rushed to join the army. They wanted to fight for freedom. Even some who were already free fought to end slavery for other blacks. Still others who joined the Union side were slaves who had run away. They fought so that they would never again be slaves.

Black Soldiers in Action

8   Nearly 200,000 black soldiers fought for the Union army. They fought in 39 large battles and in hundreds of small ones. They fought in all parts of the country. Blacks also served in the Navy. In fact, one out of four sailors was black.

9   One famous Civil War battle took place in South Carolina. A black regiment called the 54th Massachusetts attacked Fort Wagner in July 1863. The battle was a bloody defeat for the 54th. Against heavy odds, the soldiers fought bravely. In spite of their courage,

The all-black 54th Massachusetts showed great courage at Fort Wagner, in South Carolina. But the regiment lost the battle and more than 1,500 soldiers.

more than 1,500 blacks were killed. One black soldier, William H. Carney, carried the regiment's flag. He was shot several times but never dropped the banner he held proudly. Carney was later given the Medal of Honor. He was one of 16 black soldiers to win this medal during the Civil War.

10   Black soldiers fought in many other bloody battles as well. At Port Hudson, Louisiana, more than 600 of them died. Many more were killed at Fort Pillow, Tennessee. Only a few survived the vicious [vĭsh´ əs]

Black and white Union soldiers took the same risks in the Civil War. But blacks received far less pay than whites did.

fighting there. At Petersburg, Virginia, a black unit got trapped while trying to rescue[4] a white unit. Many blacks died in the struggle.

Unfair Treatment

11　Black soldiers were paid about half of what white soldiers of the same rank earned. They felt that the separate pay rates were unfair. "[Are] we soldiers," they asked, "or are we laborers? We have done a soldier's duty. Why can't we have a soldier's pay?"

---

[4] rescue: save from danger

12   General Ben Butler agreed with that thinking. "The [black man] fills an equal space in the ranks while he lives," said Butler, "and an equal grave when he falls." In 1864, the Union granted equal pay to all soldiers.

13   In all, 37,638 black soldiers died during the Civil War. It was a huge sacrifice[5] of human life. As Lincoln said, the Union could not have won the war without the black soldiers. And slavery would not have ended without that victory.

QUESTIONS

1. How did the Emancipation Proclamation change the purpose of the war?
2. Why did the Union army turn away black volunteers at first?
3. Why were blacks finally allowed to fight for the Union forces?
4. How did black soldiers feel about their rate of pay before 1864? Why?
5. About how many blacks fought for the Union during the Civil War? About how many died in the war?

---

[5] sacrifice: something offered in exchange for something else of higher value

THE THREAT OF MOUNT RAINIER

What danger hides in Mount Rainier?

1 The millions of people who live near Mount Rainier [rā nîr′] agree that it is beautiful. Its ice-capped peak stands out against the skyline. Some people climb it. Others just love to look at it. But danger hides here. Should people be warned?

2 Mount Rainier rises in the state of Washington. It is 14,410 feet high—the highest mountain in the Cascade [kăs kād′] Range. The mountain is part of a national park. Many tourists visit the park each year. They want to see the trees and the meadows filled with flowers. The tourists also come to see elk, bears, bobcats, deer, and mountain goats. But these charms are not all that Mount Rainier holds.

Mount Rainier National Park is home to more than 130 kinds of birds and 50 kinds of animals.

When it erupted in 1980, Mount St. Helens blew steam and ash about 60,000 feet into the air.

3   For Mount Rainier is not just a handsome mountain. It is also a volcano. In fact, it is part of a chain of volcanoes. Another mountain in the chain is Mount St. Helens. That mountain erupted[1] in 1980 and killed 57 people. What would happen if Mount Rainier erupted? Would even more people die?

---

[1] erupted: exploded; forced lava out

Will It Erupt?

4 Mount Rainier last erupted about 150 years ago. Scientists don't think it will erupt again soon. Even so, they can't be sure. Mount Rainier is still an active volcano. With active volcanoes, the question is when—not if— they will erupt.

5   An eruption of Mount Rainier would be quite dangerous. A small blast would not be serious. But a huge one might be terrible. It could cause more harm than Mount St. Helens did. One reason is that Mount Rainier has

A blowup of Mount Rainier could do much harm to these Tacoma buildings and homes.

very steep slopes. Lava[2] and mud would flow down the mountain. People nearby would have to get away fast.

6   Mount Rainier is also covered with ice and snow. The ice is permanent. In fact, Mount Rainier has many major glaciers[3] [glā′shərz]. A large eruption would move the glaciers down the mountain. The movement would cause huge mud slides. These mud slides could destroy anything in their paths.

7   Unlike Mount St. Helens, Mount Rainier is close to many homes and businesses. Seattle is just 65 miles away. But Tacoma is much closer. Several smaller towns are closer still. The eruption of Mount Rainer could do a lot of harm.

Living with Danger

8   Few people think that Mount Rainier will erupt soon. The streets of nearby towns are not lined with For Sale signs. People don't give the problem much thought. "If I see plumes[4] of smoke coming out of Rainier," said one man, "I might start to worry."

---

[2] lava: hot, melted rock
[3] glacier: a huge body of slow-moving ice
[4] plume: something that looks like a feather

Mount Rainier attracts nearly 10,000 hikers each year.

9   Some people guess that the mountain will erupt someday. But they do not worry about it. Says one man, "Worrying is a waste of time."

10   Others simply like living near the mountain. They think it is worth the risk. "All I think about," says one woman, "is its beauty."

Being Prepared

11   In 1994, scientists found reason to worry about Mount Rainier. Their study said that a big eruption could kill many people. It could also ruin many businesses.

12   The scientists asked people to do three things. First, they asked them to watch for seismic[5] [sīz′mĭk] activity. Second, they asked people to get ready in case the mountain erupts. For example, schools should plan how to get students out quickly. Third, they asked people to stop putting buildings so close to the mountain.

13   What will happen next? Will Mount Rainier still be a peaceful place to hike? Or will it blow up? If it does, people might use the mountain's other name: Tacoma Volcano. ◆

---

[5] seismic: caused by an earthquake or vibration of the earth

QUESTIONS

1. Why do people visit Mount Rainier?
2. Why is it hard to guess what will happen to Mount Rainier?
3. Why is Mount Rainier's ice cap a threat?
4. If Mount Rainier exploded, what else would probably happen?
5. What can people do to make the area safer?

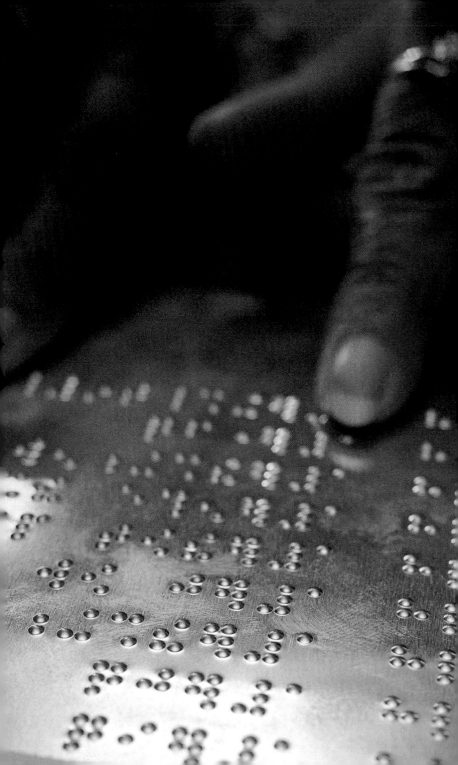

Louis Braille's Magic Dots

• • • • • • • •

How do blind people read and write?

1 In 1800, blind children had no way of learning to read. How could they? They could not see the printed page. Few parents sent their blind children to school. The children who did go to school missed much. They learned only what they could hear.

2   Louis Braille [loo͞ ē̄ brāl] was one such child. He was born in 1809 and lived in a small town near Paris, France. As a baby, Louis could see perfectly. But something awful happened when he was three years old. Louis went into his father's workshop and began to play with the tools. In a freak accident, Louis blinded himself.

Blind people read by running their fingertips along raised dots on paper.

35

A Surprise

3 When he was old enough, Louis entered the town school. No one really expected him to learn much. The teachers let Louis sit quietly in the back of the classroom.

Louis Braille (1809–1852) invented a sytem of reading and writing for the blind.

4 Louis surprised people—he learned more than the other students. He was soon at the top of his class. Still, he could not read or write. Louis might end up begging on the streets. That was a common fate for the blind.

Life at a Paris School

5 Luck was with Louis. He did not become a beggar. At age ten, he received a scholarship to a school in Paris. The school, set up for blind boys, was one of the first of its kind.

6 Students at the school learned useful skills to help them earn a living. For example, they learned to make seats for chairs and to make slippers. Once a week, the boys were taken for a walk in the park. To keep the boys from danger, the teachers linked them together by

a long rope. Life at the school was not easy. The rooms were cold and damp. The boys tried hard to follow all the rules. Teachers beat students who made trouble. Then they locked up the boys and fed them only stale bread and water.

Reading Problems

7   Reading was part of the school program. With their fingertips, students felt raised letters stamped on paper. They read by feeling letter after letter. It was a slow and difficult task. It was hard to tell one letter apart from another.

This young student learning braille looks as if she's catching on! The average reading speed is about 125 words per minute.

8   This system had an added flaw: it did not help blind students write. Special tools were needed to form the letters and stamp them onto the paper. Without them, blind students could not learn to write for themselves.

A System for Soldiers

9   One day a French soldier named Charles Barbier [bär′ bē ā] came to the Paris school. He had worked out a way for soldiers to read and write in the dark. Soldiers in night combat could send and get messages without talking. The silence kept their places on the battlefield a secret. Barbier called his system "night writing." He hoped it would be useful to blind people.

10   With night writing, words were formed by dots instead of letters. Different groups of dots stood for different sounds. Each group of dots was called a "cell." By using a simple tool, the soldiers could write on paper.

Improving Barbier's System

11   Louis Braille saw that Barbier's system was good. But it had drawbacks. For one thing, it was too slow. Each cell had as many as 12 dots. So a person had to run a finger up and down the page to feel all the dots in one cell. It was also confusing to have cells stand for sounds instead of letters.

12   Young Louis thought he could do better. He spent three years working out a new plan. By age 15, he had succeeded. His

system used only six dots per cell. The dots were much like the six dots of a domino, but smaller. Using fewer dots per cell saved a lot of space. Now a person could feel each cell with one touch of a finger. Reading became much quicker. What's more, each cell stood for a letter, not a sound. So readers could be sure of what they were reading.

A Slow Start

13 Louis became a teacher at the school where he had studied. He taught his system, simply called *braille,* to the blind students there. In his spare time, Louis worked to expand the braille system. He added math symbols and a code for writing musical notes.

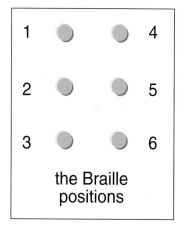

the Braille positions

14 In 1827, the first book in braille was printed. Even so, Louis's system was not widely used. One teacher at the Paris school even forbade[1] his students to learn it.

---

[1] forbade: did not allow

15   Louis Braille did not live to see his system become a success. He had struggled for years with his health, and at age 43 he died. Only a few people were left to carry on Braille's work.

Braille Catches On

16 In 1868, four English-speaking blind men got together. They knew about Braille's work. They thought braille was the key to helping other blind persons like themselves. To be on their own, the blind need to read and write. The four men began to publish books in braille. Their company became the Royal National Institute for the Blind. Today, this group prints more braille books than any other in Europe.

17   The braille system grew more and more popular. In the 1890s, a man named Frank Hall built a braille typewriter. In 1916, the United States adopted Louis Braille's system. Today, braille is used all over the English-speaking world. It has also been adapted[2] to most other written languages.

_____

[2] adapted: made suitable

A braille typewriter, or brailler, allows blind people to write.

A National Hero

18 France now praises Louis Braille for his great work. Braille's body was moved to Paris in 1952. It was buried with other French national heroes. In Braille's hometown, a monument in his honor reads "To Braille." It is signed "The Grateful Blind."

line 1	a	b	c	d	e	f	g	h	i	j
	1	2	3	4	5	6	7	8	9	0

line 2	k	l	m	n	o	p	q	r	s	t

line 3	u	v	x	y	z	and	for	of	the	with

line 4	ch	gh	sh	th	wh	ed	er	ou	ow	w

line 5	,	;	:	.	en	!	( )	"/?	in	"

line 6	st	ing	#	ar	'	-

line 7	general accent sign	used for two-celled contractions		italic sign; decimal point	letter sign	capital sign

1 ● ● 4
2 ● ● 5
3 ● ● 6

the Braille positions

**From the 6 positions of the braille cell,
63 patterns can be formed.**

QUESTIONS

1. How did Louis Braille lose his sight?
2. What was school like for Louis?
3. What was "night writing"?
4. How did Louis Braille improve on Charles Barbier's system?
5. What happened to Louis's system after his death?

The Persian Gulf War began when Iraq invaded Kuwait in 1990.

A One-Sided War

*Why did the United States go to war
in the Persian Gulf in 1991?*

1 At 2:00 A.M. on August 2, 1990, Iraq invaded[1]
Kuwait [kŏŏ wāt′]. It wasn't much of a fight.
The Iraqis crushed the small Kuwaiti army.
By sundown, the invasion [ĭn vā′ zhən] was
completed. Iraq had taken over the capital,
Kuwait City. Now people waited to see what
the United States and its allies[2] would do.

A Look Back

2 Why would Iraq strike Kuwait? There was
one reason: oil. Kuwait is located on the
Persian Gulf. It has miles of sand. There is
little to fight over. But beneath that sand is
a sea of oil. Iraq has a lot of its own oil. But
Saddam Hussein [sä däm′ hŏŏ sän′], the
leader of Iraq, wanted Kuwait's oil too.

---

[1] invaded: entered by force to conquer or overrun
[2] allies: friends; those joined in a special friendship

45

3   Iraq had just fought a long war against Iran. Wars, of course, cost money. When the price of oil was high, Iraq had money. But when the price dropped, Iraq was in trouble.

Saddam Hussein became president of Iraq in 1979.

4   Kuwait had a different problem. It made money from oil too. But it also made money in other countries. Those countries needed oil. If oil cost too much, the countries would lose money. Then Kuwait would lose money too. So Kuwait sold its oil at a very low price. This caused the price of Iraq's oil to fall. Hussein warned Kuwait to raise its price. When Kuwait said no, Iraq attacked. After taking over Kuwait, Hussein had what he wanted. With so much oil, he could keep the price high on his own.

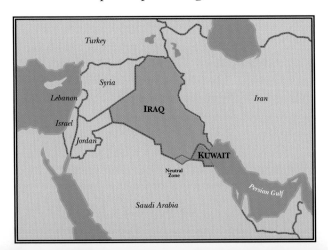

The United States Reacts

5 Hussein hoped that the United States would not complain. But he was wrong. The attack on Kuwait shocked people around the world. They worried about getting oil. Many nations depend on oil from the Persian Gulf.

6 The attack made U.S. president George Bush angry. He warned that Iraq's attack "would not stand."

7 But Bush did not want to act alone. This fight was not only between Iraq and the United States. He wanted to show that the rest of the world was angry at Iraq too. So Bush asked other allies to join in a coalition[3] [kō ə lǐsh′ən] against Iraq. Twenty-eight nations took part in it. Many other countries in the United Nations called Iraq's actions wrong.

Tension Builds

8 From the start, Bush told Iraq to get out of Kuwait. Hussein refused. He thought he would look weak if he did what Bush wanted. Instead, Hussein got even tougher. On August 8, he made Kuwait a part of Iraq. He also sent more soldiers to Kuwait.

---

[3] coalition: an agreed-upon union between nations for a special cause

9   Meanwhile, the United States got its army ready. Strong support came from U.S. allies. The United Kingdom and France sent soldiers, guns, and planes. Germany and Japan offered to help pay for them. Even the Soviet Union and China helped. Many of Kuwait's Arab neighbors helped too. Saudi Arabia, for example, let the coalition use its land. Months passed. World leaders pressed Iraq. Hussein refused to budge. Both sides kept building up their armies. At last, the U.N. sent out a final warning: Iraq had to get out of Kuwait or *else*. The deadline was January 15, 1991.

War Breaks Out

10   The deadline came and went. Hussein would not leave Kuwait. On January 16, allied planes began bombing. They used their best weapons and hit targets in Kuwait and Iraq.

11   The air attacks went on for a few weeks. They were meant to weaken the Iraqis. Leaders thought these attacks would save American lives. Sooner or later, the allies had to attack on the ground. So the weaker the Iraqis were, the better.

Allied ground troops used weapons like this short cannon, or howitzer, to strike Iraqi targets.

12   The plan worked. On February 24, the allies attacked by land and air. They broke through Iraq's line of defense. Then they moved behind Iraq's soldiers. That cut off their escape route. Thousands of Iraqi soldiers panicked. They threw down their guns. Others were captured or killed. Within four days, the war was over. The coalition had crushed Iraq. Kuwait was free.

The Costs of the War

13   The war was a disaster for Iraq. Its army was badly hurt. Many Iraqi soldiers died, and

even more were injured. Iraq also lost many tanks and planes.

14   Civilians[4] also died. The war wrecked hospitals, sewers, and food as well. Such destruction [dǐ strŭk′shən] caused many more deaths in the months after the war.

15   Most important, Iraq lost Kuwait.

16   The cost of war was also high for Kuwait. Many Kuwaiti civilians died when Iraq ruled the country. When the Iraqis knew they were beaten, they took revenge. They looted Kuwait City. Then they set fire to oil wells.

This is how Kuwait City's market area looked after the war.

---

[4] civilian: a person not in the armed forces

Oil fires are hard to put out. So Kuwait's air was black with smoke for a very long time.

Iraqi forces set fire to most of Kuwait's oil wells.

17   The war did little harm to the coalition forces. About 150 soldiers died in battle. The coalition lost fewer than 40 planes and 100 tanks.

18   Six weeks after it began, the Persian Gulf War was over. It was one of the most one-sided wars ever. ◈

QUESTIONS

1. Why did Iraq invade Kuwait?
2. What happened in other countries when Iraq took over Kuwait?
3. Name four nations that fought against Iraq.
4. Why did coalition forces drop bombs before attacking on the ground?
5. List some of the damages of the war.

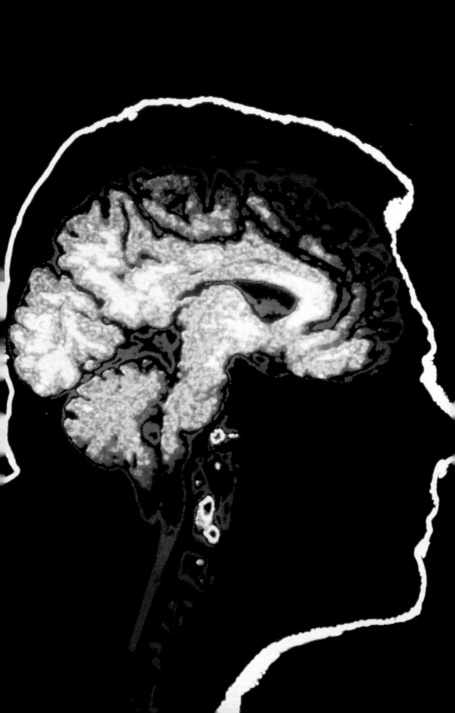

What We Know About
Memory

Can a person's memory improve?

1 What did you have for dinner last Friday? Who won last year's Super Bowl? Can you name your childhood friends? Don't be surprised if you can't. No one's memory is perfect.

Not a Simple System

2 Scientists don't know just how memory works. But the brain stores facts in a complex[1] way. First the information goes

---

[1] complex: not simple; hard to understand

The way the brain sorts and stores information is far from simple.

deep into the brain. Then it is stored as part of a pattern. These patterns lie in different parts of the brain.

3   So far, the system sounds clear. But the patterns are not. For example, nouns are stored away from verbs. The brain stores the names of things made by people in one place. But the names of natural things, like plants, are stored in another. No one has found out why this is so.

Making Memories

4   Some memories are stronger than others right from the start. You will have stronger memories of things you think are important. It is easier to remember things learned right before going to sleep. And you will remember happy times better than sad ones.

5   What do you know right now? It's easy to learn more about things you know already. Your brain lets you link one memory with another. For example, pretend that you and a friend read the same book. It is about a famous dancer. Before reading the book, your friend knows nothing about dance. But you know a great deal about it.

6   Your friend will have a hard time remembering facts from the book. Your friend's brain has no special place for dance facts. But your prior[2] knowledge will help you remember what you read. You can connect new facts with old ones. Hooking new facts onto the old ones makes stronger memories.

Words to Remember

7   Many experts say that there are five types of memory. One type includes all the words you know, even ones you haven't used in years. It also includes symbols. A dollar sign and the logo of a sports team are symbols. This type of memory also helps you remember

---

[2] prior: earlier in time or order

basic traits of things. An example would be the difference between the look of a cat and that of a dog.

8   This kind of memory is hard to lose. This is true even of people with Alzheimer's [ôlts´ hī mərz] disease. They may lose most of their other kinds of memory. But about half of them hang on to this kind.

Other Types of Memory

9   A second type of memory has to do with physical skills. Tying your shoe, for example, uses this kind of memory. You don't stop and think about each move-ment. Yet your hands do the right things in the right order.

10   A third type of memory is made up of facts. This kind holds things learned at school. It also stores things learned from movies, books, and friends. Quiz-show win-ners are people who remember facts well.

11   The shortest-term memory type lasts only a few seconds. It deals with what is going on at the moment. It remembers the start of a sentence while the speaker gets to its end. It also lets people do several things at once. You use short-term memory when you talk and watch TV while keeping your train of thought.

12   The last type of memory concerns events from your recent[3] past. These are memories of what you wore yesterday and where you ate lunch. As people age, these memories fade the most.

Sharpen Your Wits

13   Older people tend to forget things easily. But people of all ages want to remember  things better. Some wish they could recall the names of people they meet. Others want to do well on a test. Still others complain that they forget birthdays or lunch dates.

---

[3] recent: of a short time ago

14　　The good news is that you can improve your memory. One way is called *reinforcement*.[4] Try this. The next time you meet someone, say his or her name. Use the name several times as you talk with that person. This practice will create a stronger memory of the name.

15　　You can also exercise your brain. Just as exercise tones the muscles, learning improves the mind. Take a course in something you like. Study a second language. Even time spent with quick-thinking people might sharpen your wits.

16　　Many people rely on memory aids, or mnemonics [nĭ mŏn′ĭks]. One aid is a word whose letters stand for things you want to remember. To remember the names of the Great Lakes, for example, use HOMES. Each letter stands for one of the five lakes.

17　　No system is foolproof—people will still forget things. Maybe someday there will be a memory pill. In the meantime, just look up the winner of last year's game. You may *never* remember what you had for dinner last Friday! ◆

---

[4] reinforcement: giving added strength or force to an idea

QUESTIONS

1. How do scientists think the brain stores memories?
2. How can what you know already help you remember new facts?
3. What are the five types of memory?
4. Which type of memory is hard to lose?
5. Name two ways to improve your memory.

Danger in the water: THE SEA WASP

What makes a sea wasp so dangerous?

1 Six-year-old Anna Tory was splashing in the water off the Australian coast. All at once, she began to scream in pain. She had just been stung by a jellyfish. It was no ordinary jellyfish. It was a sea wasp, the most poisonous creature on Earth. Over the past 100 years, the sea wasp's venom[1] has killed dozens of people.

The Murdering Hand

2 The sea wasp goes by many names. Some people call it a box jellyfish. Others call it a

_____
[1] venom: poison produced by an animal

61

marine stinger. Its real name is *Chironex fleckeri* [kī′ rŏn ĕks flĕ′ kə rē]. *Chironex* is a blend of Greek and Latin terms. It means "murdering hand." *Fleckeri* comes from Hugo Flecker, the doctor who helped to identify the creature.

3   Before Flecker, *Chironex* victims did not know what had stung them. They could not see the pale-blue jellyfish in the blue-green ocean water. They thought they had been attacked by a sea insect. That's why they called it a sea wasp.

The Arms of Death

4   The *Chironex* is called a box jellyfish because its body is square. The body itself may grow to the size of a basketball. The *Chironex* has four eyes, one on each side of its body. These eyes puzzle scientists because a jellyfish has no brain. No one knows how it can understand messages from its eyes.

5   Still, the eyes seem to help the *Chironex*. When it sees something in its path, it turns and moves away. That explains why it does not bump into rocks and other objects.

6   Most amazing are the creature's arms. These arms, called tentacles [tĕn′ tə kəlz], are

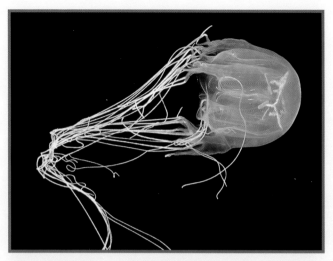

The sea wasp's long tentacles can quickly wrap around a victim. Poison shot from the many stingers on each tentacle is what kills the creature's prey.

thin. Each one is only about a fourth of an inch thick. But they are long, growing to 15 feet. There are about 60 tentacles on a single sea wasp.

7   The tentacles are covered with billions of stingers. The stingers are very close together. There may be thousands of them in a space the size of a pinhead. It is the great number of stingers that makes this jellyfish so dangerous. A bee might sting something once. A snake or spider may bite a couple of times. But the sea wasp can shoot poison from each of its stingers. So it can sting a creature billions of times in a few seconds.

Stingers in Action

8 The sea wasp lives near Australia and south-
eastern Asia. It does not attack on purpose.
Instead, it bobs gently through shallow
waters. Its long tentacles hang down below
it. If these tentacles touch a living thing, a
reaction takes place. The tentacles sense
protein[2] on the skin of the creature. The
protein excites the stingers, causing them
to release their poison.

---

[2] protein: an important building block in all living matter

9   Scientists think they know why the *Chironex fleckeri* needs such deadly venom. The creature feeds mostly on prawns[3] and shrimp. Many prawns have spikes on their tails and shells. The spikes could shred the sea wasp's soft body.

10   This means a sea wasp can't eat a prawn that is thrashing around. The prawns must be dead before the sea wasp brings them to its mouth. For its own safety, the sea wasp needs venom that can kill quickly.

11   The system works well on fish. It also works on prawns and shrimp—and humans. Venom enters the body through the skin and causes great pain. One diver said that it felt like the thrust of a hot poker through her cheek. One man's arm felt as if it had been branded with red-hot steel. Another victim said it was like having a bucket of fire poured over him. Within seconds, victims are in serious trouble.

12   The venom soon affects breathing and attacks the heart. The flow of blood slows or stops. In just four minutes, a victim can die.

---

[3] prawn: a shrimplike creature

Fighting Back

13   For years, humans were helpless in the face of the sea wasp's poison. Contact with a few inches of tentacle caused great pain. It also scarred the skin. Contact with 10 feet of tentacle was much worse. It often led to the person's death.

14   In 1970, an antivenin[4] was made. It could keep victims from dying if they got it in time. This medicine was a big step forward, but it was not enough. Remember that the venom can kill in just a few minutes. So most victims would never get the antivenin. They would be dead before reaching the hospital.

15   Another discovery came in 1979. A doctor figured out how to buy victims more time. Dr. Robert Hartwick found that vinegar kills the stinging cells of the sea wasp.

An Odd Lifesaver

16   Today many swimmers in Australia carry plenty of vinegar with them to the beach. Luckily, Anna Tory's mother had some on hand. She pulled a bottle out of her bag as soon as she saw that her daughter had been

---

[4] antivenin: a medicine that makes venom less harmful

stung. She quickly doused[5] Anna's legs and arms with it. Then she rushed the little girl to the hospital. It was a close call. Anna could barely breathe. Her heart was under great stress. Quickly, the doctors gave her the antivenin. By the end of the day, she was out of danger.

17   Back in the ocean, the sea wasp was still swimming and floating. It waited for the next meal to cross its path. Silent and hard to see, the deadly sea wasp surprises many creatures in the sea.

QUESTIONS

1. What are some other names for the sea wasp?
2. Why is a sea wasp more dangerous than a bee?
3. What happens to the human body after a sea wasp sting?
4. Why does a sea wasp need such deadly venom?
5. How can vinegar protect swimmers?

---

[5] doused: soaked

Coretta Scott King:

The Dream Lives On

Why has Coretta Scott King won a place in the hearts of many Americans?

1 Coretta Scott King is a special woman. She was married to one of the great civil rights leaders of all time, Dr. Martin Luther King, Jr. Coretta Scott King helped him in many ways and was often at his side. After King's death, she became a leader in her own right.

Early Years

2 Coretta Scott was born in Alabama in 1927. Her father ran a small store. The store did not bring in enough money to support the family. To make ends meet, Scott's father hauled

In a rare photo, **Coretta Scott King and Martin Luther King, Jr.** sit down to a family dinner at home.

lumber as a second job. Her mother worked, too, driving a school bus. Even young Scott pitched in. She picked cotton to earn money.

3   In some ways, life was hard for Scott. Each day she had to walk five miles to school. Harder still was the sight of a school bus passing her by. The bus was filled with white children. Because Scott was African American, she was not allowed to ride the bus. Such unfair treatment stung her. Someday, she vowed, people would treat her as an equal.

Unfair treatment caused Scott to value equal rights for all people.

A Good Education

4   All the students in Scott's high school were African American. Some of the teachers were white, and others were black. These teachers were the first college graduates that Scott had known. She saw that people with education had more choices in life. They were treated

with respect. Scott decided that going to college would improve her life.

5   Scott studied hard to make her dream come true. She finished first in her high school class and went on to Antioch College in Yellow Springs, Ohio. Scott studied to be a teacher but also took courses in music. She had a lovely voice and played the piano with ease.

Career Choices

6   Scott did well in college. But when it was time to do some practice teaching, she had a letdown.[1] Antioch students always did their practice teaching at the Yellow Springs public schools. But no African American had ever taught in the public schools. So Scott was sent to the school run by the college.

7   Scott's race had become an issue [ĭsh′ o͞o] once again. It kept her from getting the same training that her white classmates got. Scott decided not to become a teacher after all. She went on with her studies in music. After college, Scott moved to Boston and enrolled[2] in a top music school. She did not have much money. For a time, she lived on graham

---

[1] letdown: something that spoils a person's hope
[2] enrolled: signed up

crackers, peanut butter, and fruit. Still, she was happy to be doing something she loved.

Fighting For Equal Rights

8   In Boston, Scott met Martin Luther King, Jr., who was also a student. The two of them talked about their hopes for the future. Their goals in life were very much the same. Both Scott and King wanted to help African Americans win equal rights. They hoped to end the suffering that came from racial[3] prejudice [prĕj′ ə dĭs].

Martin Luther King, Jr., gives his famous "I Have a Dream" speech after the 1963 civil rights march in Washington, D.C.

---

[3] racial: having to do with dealings between people of different races

9   In 1953, Scott and King married. The next year, when they finished school, they moved to Alabama. The year after that, the first of their four children was born. In 1956, King helped launch[4] a bus boycott[5] in Montgomery, Alabama. The goal was to end poor treatment of blacks on city buses. The boycott went on for a year. By the time it ended, King was famous. From then on, he was a leader in the civil rights movement.

Living with Danger

10   King's work stirred the feelings of many white people. Some of them agreed with him, but others did not. A few of King's enemies even wanted to get rid of him. One day someone threw a bomb at the King home. Luckily, no one was hurt. But it was clear that the King family was a target for angry whites.

11   Over the next 12 years, Coretta Scott King feared for the safety of her family. Still, she and her husband went on with their civil rights work. King was in the public eye more and more. He gave speeches and set up marches. Through the years, Scott King often

---

[4] launch: start
[5] boycott: a plan to not deal with a person, company, or country to force better terms

The 1965 march in Montgomery, Alabama, drew much attention to the civil rights movement. Can you find singers Harry Belafonte and Tony Bennett, and actor Anthony Perkins marching with the Kings?

marched beside her husband. She sometimes spoke in his place when he had to miss a speaking date. On tours of the United States and abroad,[6] she was at King's side. At the meetings, she often sang about civil rights. In 1964, Scott King talked about her family's life. She knew they lived "on the edge of danger." She said, "People constantly ask Martin and

---

[6] abroad: in or to countries far away

In 1968, Coretta Scott King founded the King Center in Atlanta, Georgia. It was built in memory of Dr. King and works for social change without violence.

me how we can hope to raise normal, healthy and happy children. . . ." Her answer was simple. She said, "I can only answer that we have faith in God and that we try to be good parents."

Carrying On

12   On April 4, 1968, Martin Luther King, Jr., was shot and killed. Scott King bravely carried on her husband's work. She gave the speeches

that he had planned to give. She took his place at a march planned long before.

13   To honor his memory, Scott King created the King Center. It includes King's childhood home and his tomb. The Atlanta church where King worked is also part of the center.

14   More than three million people visit the King Center each year. Although the center has kept Scott King busy, she has found time for other human rights work. She has spoken at peace rallies. She has also given many freedom concerts. Her words and songs keep alive the struggle against racism, poverty, and

In this recent photo, Coretta Scott King speaks about the progress of the human rights movement.

war. In 1994, she led a march on Washington, D.C., just as her husband had done more than 30 years before.

15   By her words and actions, Coretta Scott King has won a place in the hearts of many Americans. People will always remember her as the wife of Martin Luther King, Jr. But she will also be honored for her own strength, grace, and dignity.[7]

QUESTIONS

1. What problems did Coretta Scott face as a young girl?
2. Why did Coretta Scott move to Boston?
3. What dreams did Coretta Scott and Martin Luther King, Jr., share?
4. What did Coretta Scott King do after her husband's death?

---

[7] dignity: a state of being worthy or respected

HOW TO SURVIVE ANYTHING

*Can you keep your cool in the
face of danger?*

1 It's a dangerous world out there. Life is full of close calls. You might some day find yourself in one of the following jams. Here are ways to make it through in one piece—with a smile on your face.

Calm a Mad Dog

2 You're out walking. You hear the bark of an angry dog behind you.

THE BASICS.

3 1. Animals are not kind.
2. If you panic, they panic.
3. If they panic, they bite.

How would you stay in one piece if this hound were after you?

THE DETAILS.

4   *You will want to run.* Don't. Almost two million people are bitten by dogs each year. You can't outrun most dogs. Most of the time, the dog is angry because you are on its turf. It is trying to scare you off.

5   *Play on the dog's terms.* Stand still. Turn and face the dog. Don't make any quick movements. Talk in a quiet voice. This shows the dog you're not a threat. The dog should calm down. When it does, back away slowly. Keep watching the dog.

6   *Throw the dog a bone.* Do you have some food in your pocket? Share it. The old saying is true—a dog is not likely to bite the hand that feeds it.

7   *What if this doesn't work?* If the dog doesn't calm down, try to show it you're the boss. Stand as tall as you can. Scream and stare it in the eye. Take off your jacket or sweater. Wrap it around your fist. If the dog comes at you, offer your protected fist. Back off slowly, taking the dog with you. When you reach a safe place, let go of the clothing.

8   What if the dog is a strong one, such as a Doberman? You don't think you can fight it off? Curl into a ball with your hands over

your head. The dog may still bite you.
But your throat and other vital[1] parts are
protected.

Make It Through a Storm at Sea

9   There's an old joke about getting seasick:
First you're afraid you're going to die. Then
you're afraid you won't. From birth, people
are used to solid ground. A rocking boat
throws the system off balance.

A sailor could lose more than his lunch during this bad storm.

---

[1] vital: necessary for life to go on

10 **THE BASICS.**

1. Go with the motion of the ocean.
2. Don't eat grease before you sail.
3. Stay in the middle of the boat.

THE DETAILS.

11 *Deny everything.* Don't worry about getting seasick, and there's a good chance you won't.

12 *Watch what you eat.* Don't eat a lot before boarding the boat. Stick with mild foods like crackers. Drink plenty of water, and avoid alcohol and greasy foods.

13 *Never go below.* Stay on deck. If you go below, the room will seem to be standing still. But your sense of balance will tell you you're moving. That can make you seasick.

14 *Eat ginger.*[2] Ginger seems to soothe the stomach. Try ginger ale or ginger tablets or even ginger snaps.

15 *Take medicine early.* You can buy medicine at the drugstore to prevent seasickness. But it will help only if you take it before you feel sick. There is a patch you can wear to prevent seasickness. But your doctor must prescribe[3] [prĭ skrīb'] it for you.

---

[2] ginger: a thick underground plant stem used to make a spice and sometimes used in medicine

[3] prescribe: order or direct the use of something as a medicine

Plan your escape before you need to make it.

Escape a Towering Inferno [4]

16 It's fun to watch a disaster movie. But
nobody wants to star in his or her own
disaster. If you're in a tall building that
catches fire, there are a few things you
need to know.

---

[4] inferno: a place or state that relates to hell, usually with
great heat or raging fire

THE BASICS.

17 1. Stay out of elevators.

2. Stay down low.

3. Close the door against fire.

THE DETAILS.

18 *Plan your getaway.* The tall building may be the office you go to every day. Or it may be your apartment house. It may even be a hotel you are visiting. Find out where the fire escapes are. Hotels have maps in every room. Most offices and apartments also have maps. Plan at least two ways to get out. If you're in a hotel, count the room doors between your room and the fire escape. If the fire happens at night and you can't see, this will help you find your way.

19 *Step lively.* Get out as quickly as you can. Use smoke-free stairways. Never use the elevator.

20 *Lie low.* If a room or hall is full of smoke, crawl on your hands and knees. The best air is 12 to 24 inches from the floor. You can also see better there. If you can, put a wet cloth over your mouth and nose. This will help filter out the smoke.

21 *If you're trapped.* If you're trapped in a room, call the fire department. Tell them where you

are. If the phones are out, get a flashlight and signal from the window. Or you can hang a light-colored sheet or towel out the window. Fill the bathtub with water. Soak towels in the water. Stuff them in cracks around the door and seal vents with them. Turn off any fans or air conditioners.

Stop Yourself from Choking

22 Choking is not the way a person expects to die. But it kills people more often than you think. If you get something stuck in your windpipe, don't wait around for help.

T H E   B A S I C S .

23 All you need to know is how to do the Heimlich maneuver [hīm′ lĭk mə nōō′ vər]. First make a fist. Put the thumb side against your upper abdomen [ăb′ də mən] just below

Done correctly, the Heimlich maneuver can save a person's life.

your rib cage. Hold the fist with your other hand. Push hard in and up at the same time. The food should fly out of your mouth.

24   If that doesn't work, lean over the back of a chair. The edge should stick into your abdomen. Push yourself quickly down on it. This should force the air out of your diaphragm[5] [dī′ə frăm]. Do this until the pieces of food shoot out of your mouth.

Avoid a Car Accident

25 You don't want to look ahead and see a car coming across the road at you. But head-on crashes kill 5,000 people a year in the United States.

THE BASICS.

26 1. Swerve right! Quick!
2. A rear-end crash is better than one head-on.

THE DETAILS.

27 *Light up.* Drive with your headlights on during the day. Studies show that it helps prevent head-on crashes.

28 *Avoid skidding.* Take your foot off the brake. Steer away from trouble. At speeds higher

---

[5] diaphragm: a sheet of muscle that separates the chest from the abdomen

A wet road may have played a role in this car crash.

than 30 miles an hour, it is quicker to steer
around something than to stop your car. It
is usually safer to steer to the right. That is
because the oncoming driver will most often
steer to *his* or *her* right.

29   *Crash straight ahead.* You may not be able to
avoid some kind of accident. If you must, hit
someone driving in the same direction as you
are. It will be a less messy accident.

30   *Bounce back.* If you can't avoid hitting a tree
or a guardrail, try to hit it with the side of
your car.

31 *Use seat belts.* Wearing a seat belt is one of the best ways to protect yourself in a crash. This keeps you in the correct position behind the wheel.

If Your Brakes Give Out . . .

32 1. Pump them once or twice. See if you have any braking power.
2. If you don't have any brakes, put the car in neutral. Keep your eyes on the road ahead. Slow the car with the parking brake. But don't lock the brakes, or you will skid. If your parking brake is next to the driver's seat, keep your finger on the brake-release button. Slowly raise the brake. If your parking brake is on the floor, keep your left hand on the brake-release lever.[6] Slowly press down on the brake with your foot.
3. If that doesn't work, steer to an open field. Or let your tires rub against the curb to slow you down.

33   Life is not certain, to say the least. But with a plan, some common sense, and a little luck, you *can* survive just about anything. ◆

---

[6] lever: a bar or rod used to run or adjust something

QUESTIONS

1. About how many people are bitten by dogs each year?

2. What should you do if you can't fight off a strong dog?

3. Name two things you shouldn't eat or drink before boarding a boat.

4. If you are trapped in a room of a building on fire, why would you soak towels in water?

5. In trying to avoid a head-on car crash, in which direction should you swerve?

PHOTO CREDITS

Cover GBRMPA. **viii** © Bob Krist/ The Stock Market.
4, 5 Reuters/ Corbis-Bettmann. **7** Carole Elies/ Tony Stone
Images. **10** Pascal Crapet/ Tony Stone Images. **17** Charles
Bennett/ AP Photo. **18** Chicago Historical Society. **19** Hulton
Getty/ Tony Stone Images. **20** Lawrence D. Thornton/ Archive
Photos. **23** Tri-Star Pictures/ Shooting Star. **24** Chicago
Historical Society. **26** Chuck Pefley/ Tony Stone Images.
28 Ralph Perry/ Tony Stone Images. **29** © David Barnes/ The
Stock Market. **31** © Dave Davidson/ The Stock Market.
34 © 1992 Mark E. Gibson/ Picture Perfect USA. **36** Hulton
Getty/ Tony Stone Images. **37** Perkins School for the Blind.
41 © Robert E. Daemmrich/ Tony Stone Images. **44** *top, bottom*
Reuters/ Corbis-Bettmann; *middle* Corinne Dufka/ Reuters/
Corbis-Bettmann. **46** Jim Hollander/ Reuters/ Corbis-Bettmann.
49 Charles Platiau/ Reuters/ Corbis-Bettmann. **50** © 1991
Tomas Muscionico/ The Stock Market. **51** Peter Wenzel/ Tony
Stone Images. **52** © 1996 Howard Sochurek/ The Stock Market.
56 NTC/Contemporary Books. **60, 63** P. Hamner/ GBRMPA
61 D. McKillop/ GBRMPA. **68** Flip Schulke/ Black Star.
70 UPI/ Corbis-Bettmann. **72** Archive Photos. **74** APWire Photo.
75 © Ron Sherman/ Click Chicago. **76** AP by John Bazemore.
78 © 1996 Jon Feingersh/ The Stock Market. **81** Rex Ziak/ Tony
Stone Images. **83** Peter Timmermans/ Tony Stone Images.
85 Bruce Ayres/ Tony Stone Images. **87** © Randy O' Rourke/
The Stock Market.

ILLUSTRATIONS

Mitch Lopata